Richard Rohr, OFM, is a Franciscan priest of the New Mexico Province and Founding Director of the Center for Action and Contemplation (CAC) in Albuquerque, New Mexico. An internationally recognized author and spiritual leader, Fr. Richard teaches primarily on incarnational mysticism, non-dual consciousness, and contemplation, with a particular emphasis on how these affect the social justice issues of our time.

Along with many recorded conferences, he is the author of numerous books, including *The Universal Christ* (2019), *Just This* (2018), *The Divine Dance* (2016), *Immortal Diamond* (2013), and *Falling Upward* (2012), all published by SPCK. To learn more about Fr. Richard Rohr and the CAC, visit https://cac.org/richard-rohr/richard-rohr-ofm/.

T0324382

RICHARD ROHR
silent
compassion

finding God in
contemplation

Originally published in the United States of America in 2014
by Franciscan Media, 28 W. Liberty St., Cincinnati, OH 45202,
www.FranciscanMedia.org

Published in Great Britain in 2022

Society for Promoting Christian Knowledge
36 Causton Street
London SW1P 4ST
www.spck.org.uk

Scripture quotations are from the author's own translation.

British Library Cataloguing-in-Publication Data
A catalogue record for this book is available from the British Library

ISBN 978–0–281–08660–3

1 3 5 7 9 10 8 6 4 2

Typeset by Falcon Oast Graphic Art Ltd
Printed and bound in Great Britain by Clays Ltd, Elcograf S.p.A.

Produced on paper from sustainable sources

Contents

Preface

Different Faiths Gather to Seek True Harmony

In Louisville, Kentucky, in mid-May 2013, a group of varied religious leaders stood in front of a respectable crowd at the city's cavernous downtown Yum Convention Center. The gathering was a special day at the end of the City of Louisville's occasional Festival of Faiths, a program of public events intended to nurture interfaith dialog, to build a respectful, unified community.

There were Muslims there, Hindus, Jews, Christians, Buddhists. Richard Rohr, O.F.M., a Catholic, Franciscan priest (one among several Christian leaders present), represented Christianity. Buddhism was represented by the most famous speaker, His Holiness the Dalai Lama.

In a sense, it was fitting that these two should share a stage in Louisville. It was another Catholic priest, a Cistercian Trappist, the late Father Thomas Merton who had traveled from nearby Gethsemani, Kentucky, all the way across the world to southeast Asia for an interfaith event fifty years earlier. Days before his tragic accidental death, he was seen walking, in deep conversation with the Dalai Lama, who was then a young man at the beginning of his career.

Now, all these years later, His Holiness the Dalai Lama had come to Louisville, a stop at what, by now, had become a world tour, not only to build support for the oppressed people of Tibet, but also to spread his own message of peace, of mysticism, a blend of action and contemplation built on an ancient tradition that has so characterized his life.

Father Rohr—Richard Rohr to the many thousands who seek guidance from his many talks, books, and webcasts—devoted his life to much of the same, but from his own ancient tradition. In the mid-1980s, he founded the Center for Action and Contemplation in Albuquerque, New Mexico, to be a laboratory of sorts, from where, as thousands of socially minded Christians have learned, social activism can be informed, purified, improved through the ancient practice of contemplation.

His words fit well in the context of an interfaith gathering, for Richard has always been able to see beyond the here and now, and outside the walls that social groups build around themselves.

Of course, Richard is following in the footsteps of his own "Father Francis" known easily, worldwide, as St. Francis of Assisi. It was Francis who wandered hill and dale in central Italy around the turn of the thirteenth century. Francis went from town to town, sometimes preaching, sometimes leading merely by example, in a culture that had never seen anything quite like him. He was open to the signs of God in all of creation (he's the saint in today's birdbaths), earth, trees, flowers and animals alike, but also in every person. He is perhaps the world's most famous peacemonger, even traveling with Crusaders to Egypt to preach peace and intercultural understanding to Christians and Muslims alike. His message of peace resonates today.

Now, on those few but charged days in spring in Louisville, representatives from the world's major religions were gathered to assert and probe that same desire. How can we live together, in true harmony? How can we learn from one another? What wisdom is there for everyone in each of the traditions?

Captured for history, just a few blocks from the convention center, at the corner of Fourth and Walnut (now Muhammad Ali Boulevard), is a bronze plaque, a memorial to the pivotal point in Thomas Merton's life that he describes in *Conjectures of a Guilty Bystander.* On that corner, back in 1958, Father Merton had a mystical insight into the oneness of humanity. Looking at the bustling crowd in the center of Louisville's shopping district, he realized that the mystery of God is surrounding us at all times. "I was suddenly overwhelmed with the realization that I loved all those people, that they were mine and I theirs, that we could not be alien to one another even though we were total strangers . . . There is no way of telling people that they are all walking around shining like the sun."

Louisville's Festival of Faiths grew out of that spirit, that awareness that we all are in this together. Richard Rohr is helping us to understand that.

John Feister
Editor in Chief,
St. Anthony Messenger magazine

Introduction

The Perennial Tradition

The "perennial philosophy" or "perennial tradition" is a term that has come in and out of popularity in Western and religious history, but it has never been dismissed by the Universal Church. In many ways, it was actually affirmed at the Second Vatican Council, in its forward-looking documents on ecumenism (*Unitatis Redintegratio*) and non-Christian religions (*Nostra Aetate*). It affirms that there are some constant themes, truths, and recurrences in all the world religions.

In *Nostra Aetate,* for example, the Council Fathers begin by saying that "All peoples comprise a single community and have a single origin [created by one and the same Creator God]. And one also is their final goal: God . . . The Catholic Church rejects nothing which is true and holy in these religions."[1] Then the document goes on to praise Native religion, Hinduism, Judaism, Buddhism, and Islam as "reflecting a ray of that truth which enlightens all people."[2] You have got to realize what courage and brilliance it took to write that in 1965, when very few people in any religion thought that way. In fact, most still don't think that way today.

One early exception was the great St. Augustine (354–430), a Doctor of the Church, who courageously wrote: "The very thing which is now called the Christian religion was not wanting among the ancients from the beginning of the human race until Christ came in the flesh. After that time, the true religion, which had always existed, began to be called 'Christian.'"[3] St. Clement of Alexandria, Origen, St. Basil, St. Gregory of Nyssa, and St. Leo the Great all held similar understandings before we got into the defensive (and offensive!) modes of anti-Semitism and the Crusades. In some crucial ways, we have actually gone backward in religious history, when we should have been greasing the wheels of spiritual consciousness to move forward.

The term is approximately used in the council's decree on priestly formation (*Optatam Totius*), where it states that seminarians should "base themselves on a philosophy which is perennially valid," and the decree encourages study of the entire history of philosophy and also "recent scientific progress."[4] The authors were probably thinking primarily of Scholastic philosophy; in truth, our term, as we use it here, is much more a theological statement than a philosophical one, anyway. This is Aldous Huxley's understanding, which is why he calls it a metaphysic, a psychology, and an ethic at the same time: "1) the metaphysic which recognizes a divine Reality substantial to the world of things and lives and minds; 2) the psychology that finds in the soul something similar to, or even identical to, divine Reality; 3) the ethic that places man's final end in the knowledge of the immanent and transcendent Ground of all being. This is immemorial and universal. Rudiments of the perennial philosophy may be found among the traditional lore of primitive peoples in every region of the world, and in its fully developed forms it has a place in every one of the higher religions."[5]

The divisions, dichotomies, and dualisms of the world can only be overcome by a unitive consciousness at every level: personal, relational, social, political, cultural, in interreligious dialogue, and in spirituality in particular. This is the unique and central job of healthy religion (*re-ligio* means "to re-ligament"!).

As Jesus put it in his great final prayer, "I pray that all may be one" (John 17:21). Or, as my favorite Christian mystic, Lady Julian of Norwich (1342–1416) put it, "By myself I am nothing at all, but in general, I AM in the oneing of love. For it is in this oneing that the life of all people exists."[6]

Many teachers have made the central, but oft-missed, point that *unity is not the same as uniformity*. Unity, in fact, is the reconciliation of differences, and those differences must be maintained—and yet overcome! You must actually distinguish things and separate them before you can spiritually unite them, usually at cost to yourself (Ephesians 2:14–16). If only we had made that simple clarification, so many problems—and over-emphasized, separate identities—could have moved to a much higher level of love and service.

Paul already made this universal principle very clear in several of his letters. For example, "There is a variety of gifts, but it is always the same Spirit. There are all sorts of service to be done, but always to the same Lord, working in all sorts of different ways in different people. It is the same God working in all of them" (1 Corinthians 12:4–6). In his community at Ephesus, they were taught, "There is one Lord, one faith, one baptism, one God who is Father of all, over all, through all, and within all, and each one of us has been given his own share of grace" (Ephesians 4:5–7).

We must finally go back to the ultimate Christian source for our principle—the central doctrine of the Trinity itself. Yes, God is one, just as our Jewish ancestors taught us (Deuteronomy 6:4), and yet the further, more subtle, level is that this *oneness* is, in fact, the radical love union between three completely distinct persons of the Trinity. The basic principle and problem of the one and the many is overcome in God's very nature. God is a mystery of *relationship*, and the truest relationship is love. The three are not uniform, but quite distinct, yet completely *unified* in total outpouring!

Further, our word *person*, now referring to an individual human being, was actually first used in Greek-based Trinitarian theology (*persona* means "stage mask" or a "sounding through"), and later then applied also to us! So we also are not autonomous beings, but soundings through, apart but radically one, too, just as Father, Son, and Holy Spirit are. The implications could make for years of meditation. We really are created in God's "image and likeness" (Genesis 1:26ff), much more than we ever imagined. Trinity is our universal template for the nature of reality and for how to become one!

As dear Julian said, "The love of God creates in us such a *oneing* that when it is truly seen, no person can separate themselves from another person,"[7] and "In the sight of God all humans are *oned*, and one person is all people and all people are in one person."[8]

This is not some twenty-first-century flabby fabrication. This is not pantheism or mere New Age optimism. This is the whole point; it was, indeed, supposed to usher in a new age—and still will and can. This is the perennial tradition. Our job is not to discover it, but only to retrieve what has been discovered—and enjoyed—again and again, in the mystics and saints of all religions.

As John the Beloved said, "I do not write to you because you do not know the truth, [we] are writing to you here because you know it already" (1 John 2:21).

One

Finding God in the Depths of Silence

People who are interested in issues of peace and justice surely recognize at this point in time how communication, vocabulary, and conversation have reached a very low point in our society. I think we are aware of that in our politics, but we are aware of it in our churches, too. It feels like the only way through this is a re-appreciation for this wonderful, but seemingly harmless, thing called silence.

How do you market that which is inherently unmarketable? How do you sell silence? How do you make attractive what feels like selling air or selling emptiness or selling something that, certainly to the capitalistic mind, would not immediately be attractive at all? Let's try anyway!

Silence is not just that which is around words and underneath images and events. It has a life of its own. It's a phenomenon with almost a physical identity. It is a being in itself to which you can relate. Philosophically, we would say *being* is that foundational quality which precedes all other attributes. When you relate to the naked being of a thing, you learn to know it at its core. Silence is somehow at the very foundation of all reality. It is that out of which all being comes and to which all things return. (If the word silence does not grab you, you can interchange it with nothingness, emptiness, vastness, formlessness, open space, etc.)

What we do know is that all things are a *creatio ex nihilo*, that every something, by God's plan, first comes from nothing! If you can first rest in the nothing, you will then be prepared to appreciate the something. When nothing creates something, we call it grace!

Such silence was described in the very first two verses of the Book of Genesis. The first reality is described as a "formless void," and the Spirit is "hovering" over this silent void. The Spirit is silent but powerful. And the coming together of these two great silences is the beginning of our creation, at least in the Judeo-Christian story.

Silence precedes, undergirds, and grounds everything. We cannot just see it as an accident, or as something unnecessary. But unless we learn how to live there, go there, abide in this different phenomenon, the rest of things—words, events, relationships, identities—all become rather superficial, without depth or context. They lose meaning. All we search for is a life of more events, more situations which have to increasingly contain ever-higher stimulation, more excitement, and more color, to add vital signs to our inherently bored and boring existence. It really is the most simple and stripped down things that ironically have the power to give us the greatest happiness—*if* we respect them as such. Silence is the essence of simple and stripped down.

This need for stimulation is the character of America and most Western countries I am afraid. We must be honest about this. There are so many signs of deterioration of culture all around us. Everything has to be a little louder, a little brighter, a little newer, a little more expensive, a little classier, and especially a little quicker. And then the Americans will come. It is

2

not, "If you build it, they will come," but "If you make it fancy, they will come." And we have grown used to this. We accept as normative what even the Roman emperors knew was a sign of decline: "Bread and circuses are all this people needs or wants," they said. We close schools and build sports stadiums that look like cathedrals.

One of the most important experiences for me has been to teach in so many developing countries, where I came to the recognition that most of the world does not live the way we live. But even more sadly, they want to!

We must not think of ourselves as the norm or the goal. This is not necessarily a healthy society. We are not necessarily the best culture or the greatest, although I know Americans are trained to think that way. It is only easy to think that way if you have never been outside of America. We surely have some wonderful aspects to our society, and some very unhealthy aspects, too, including that we would not see silence as anything attractive or useful or necessary or important or even good. In time, we become more a shell with less and less inside or in the depths of things—where all the vitality is to be found.

We need to try to see silence as a living presence of itself, which is primordial and primal, and then see all other things—now experienced deeply—inside of that container. It is not just an absence, but, also by that very fact, a *presence*. Silence surrounds every "I know" event with a humble and patient "I don't know." It protects the autonomy and dignity of events, persons, animals, and all things.

We must find a way to return to this place, to live in this place, to abide in this place of inner silence. Outer silence means very little if there is not a deeper inner silence. Everything else appears much clearer as it appears or emerges out of a previous silence. And when I use the word *appear*, I mean it takes on reality, substance, significance, or meaning. Without silence around a thing, which is a mystery, nothing has meaning or meaning that lasts. It is just another event in a sequence of ever-quicker events, which we call our lives.

Without silence, we do not really experience our experiences. We have many experiences, but they do not have the power to change us, to awaken us, to give us that joy that the world cannot give, as Jesus says.

To live in this primordial, foundational being itself, which I am calling silence, creates a kind of sympathetic resonance with what is right in front of us. Without it, we just react. We are Mexican jumping beans, reacting instead of responding. Without some degree of silence, we are never living, never tasting, as there is not much capacity to enjoy, or to appreciate, or to taste the moment. *The opposite of contemplation is not action, it is reaction.* We must wait for pure action, which always proceeds from a contemplative silence.

Silence is not the absence of being, but it is a kind of being itself. It is not something distant or obtuse or obscure of which only ascetics are capable. But rather you may have already experienced deep silence, and now you must feed it and free it, and allow it to become light within you. You do not hear silence (precisely!), but it is *that by which you do hear*. You cannot capture silence. It captures you.

Silence is a kind of thinking that is not thinking. It is a kind of thinking which *sees* (*contemplata* means "to see"). Silence, then, is an alternative consciousness. It is a form of intelligence, a form of knowing beyond bodily reacting, which is what we normally call emotion. It is a form of knowing beyond mental analysis, which is what we usually call thinking.

By the age of seven, almost all of us have separated our body and our soul from our mind, and we give all of our credence to our mind, disconnected from our bodies, disconnected from our souls, which abide and grow more in silence.

Descartes was not wrong when he said, "I think therefore I am." He was accurately describing the Western person. Our thinking is who we think we are, I am sorry to report. But we are so much more than our thoughts about things.

All of the great world religions at the higher levels discovered that this tyrannical mode of thinking has to be relativized, has to be limited, or it takes over—and rather completely takes over—to the loss of primal being. And pretty soon, words mean less and less; they mean whatever we want them to mean. (We must be honest here.) But this leads to more and more cynicism and suspicion about all words, even our own. This is our post-modern culture. We all use words to mean what we want— so that we can get what we want. It is an incestuous circle.

Listen to the character of whatever political debate emerges in this country: guns, health care, war, or whatever the recent reality show is. The words on either side mean less and less in terms of objective truth, and we have all come to know this. It becomes a game that we all are forced to play. The only way out is often to be silent—like Jesus before Pilate (Mark 15:5; John 19:9).

The soul does not use words. It surrounds words with space, and that is what I mean by silence.

The ego, on the other hand, uses words to get what it wants. When we are in an argument with our spouses or friends or colleagues, that is what we do. We pull out the words that give us power. We pull out the words that make us look right, superior, and intelligent, and win the argument. We all have done it. It is all the ego knows how to do. But words at that level are rather useless and even dishonest and destructive.

The filling of space with words and sound is now called entertainment. And even there we too often focus on things that are tragic, or that will draw forth sentiment or reaction. And we call that urgent news, which we know is often manufactured by the emotion of the newscaster's voice. At that point, we are three steps removed from contact with reality.

This is what is inevitably going to happen when there is no appreciation for silence, when the silence around the words is not just as important, or even maybe more important, than the choosing of the words themselves.

Silence is a kind of wholeness. It can absorb contraries. It can absorb paradoxes and contradictions. Maybe that is why we do not like silence. There is nothing to argue about in true inner silence, and the mind likes to argue. It gives us something to do.

But often our interactions lead to argumentation, even within the Church and often about the forms of prayer itself. Take the issue of inclusive language or male or female leadership, which are indeed important questions. Do I like that psalm, or is this psalm too violent? Is that singing too Evangelical or too Catholic or too charismatic? There has to be an issue with something, or I hardly feel useful. That is one reason that contemplative prayer, especially in a group, is so liberating and calming. There are no sides to take.

It comes down to this: the ego loves something it can take sides on. And true interior silence really does not allow you to take sides. I describe this common tendency as dualistic thinking and not contemplation itself.

Now you can see how someone who lives in a capitalist culture like we do, where everything is about competing and comparing and winning, will find silence counterintuitive. How do you teach something as empty, as harmless, as certain to create failure as silence? Only when you know that it also offers a "peace beyond understanding" (Philippians 4:7) and a "joy that no one can take from you" (John 16:22).

But if those in the Church limit their focus to external technique and formula with which most liturgy becomes preoccupied (e.g., how the priests' hands are folded, what words he is saying, and what type of vestments he is wearing), the soul remains largely untouched and unchanged. Too much emphasis on what I will call "social prayer" or wordy prayer gives us far too much to argue about, and that is surely why Jesus emphasized the quiet prayer in one's own "inner room" and not to "babble on as the pagans do" (Matthew 6:5–7).

What I have experienced during my longer Lenten retreats is that time actually increases inside of silence. It feels like time "coming to fullness," as the New Testament says, time beyond time. It shifts from each successive moment of chronological time, from the Greek *chromos*, to *kairos* or momentous time, when one moment is as perfect as it can be, when it is all right here, right now, it is enough. I am more than okay. I am content.

If you can see silence as the ground of all words and the birth of all words, then you will find that when you speak, your words will be more well-chosen and calm.

Francis told us to always use words that were "well-chosen and chaste," in other words, not to preach unless we have something to say, not to preach just to be preaching. But all preaching was to be the direct fruit of contemplation, and not just idle ideas (like many of mine)!

I think that when you recognize something as beautiful in your life, it partly emerges from the silence around it. It may be why we are quiet in art galleries. If something is not surrounded by the vastness of silence and space, it is hard to appreciate something as singular and beautiful. If it is all mixed in with everything else, then its singularity, as a unique and beautiful object, does not stand out.

Silence needs to be understood in a larger way than simply a lack of audible sound or a lack of noise. Whenever emptiness—what seems like empty space, absence of sound—becomes its own kind of fullness with its own kind of sweet voice, you have just experienced what I mean by silence.

As one author I read years ago said, silence is the net below the tightrope walker. We are walking, trying to find the right words to explain our experience, but silence is that safety net that allows us to fall, that says and admits, as poets often do, that no word will ever be perfectly right or is ever sufficient. So the poet keeps trying, for which we are grateful! The great spaciousness and safety net beneath a tightrope walker is silence. It frees her or him from self-preoccupation and fear of making a mistake. The silence will uphold me and surround my mistakes and give me more space to correct them.

There are two kinds of silence. There is the natural refreshing silence of the introverted personality or the pause between conversations. But there is also a spiritual silence, a silence that does not need to be filled with nervous laughter or a joke or any attempt to be clever or show that you are informed and an insider. Such spiritual silence demands a deep presence to oneself in the moment.

If life is primarily words and ideas, and that is what we have made it into, especially after the invention of the printing press, then death—that great mystery that we haven't walked through yet—is silence. And therefore, you could say that faith and silence are both a practicing for death. Who am I before—and after—all my words and ideas and understandings?

I began my book *Immortal Diamond* with these epigraphs:

Ken Wilber says, "The fact that life and death are 'not two' is extremely difficult to grasp, not because it is so complex, but because it is so simple."

Then also an epigraph from Kathleen Dowling Singh, a hospice worker in Florida, who said, "We miss the unity of life and death at the very point where our ordinary mind begins to think about it."

Contemplation is precisely calling that ordinary mind into question and saying this thing you call thinking cannot get you there. We need a different operating system, and it both begins with silence and leads to silence.

In my book, *The Naked Now*, I called non-silence "dualistic thinking," where everything is separated into opposites, like life and death. The dualistic mind is almost the only mind left in the West. We even think it is what it means to be educated—to be

9

very good at dualistic thinking—but it is what Jesus and Buddha would call judgmental thinking (Matthew 7:1–5), and they both strongly warn us against it.

Dualistic thinking is operative almost all of the time. It is when you choose one side, or temperamentally prefer one side, and then call the other side of the equation false, wrong, heresy, or untrue. It is often something to which you have not yet been exposed, or it threatens you or your ego in a way, or is beyond your education. The dualistic mind splits the moment and forbids the dark side, the mysterious, the paradoxical. This is the common level of conversation that we have in the world. Basically, it lacks humility and patience, and it is the opposite of contemplation.

Non-dual thinking is precisely contemplation. It is not a very inspiring term for what we thought was prayer, but it is a clinically descriptive word of exactly what is happening. The Holy Spirit frees you from taking sides and allows you to remain content in the partial darkness of every situation long enough to let it teach you, broaden you, and enrich you. You have to practice for many years, and make many mistakes in the meantime, to learn how to do this. Paul beautifully speaks of it in Philippians (4:6–7): "Pray with gratitude and the peace of Christ, which is beyond knowledge or understanding ("the making of distinctions"), will guard both your mind and your heart in Christ Jesus." It is all right there in concise form. Teachers of contemplation teach you how to stand guard and not let your emotions and obsessive thoughts control you.

When you're thinking non-dualistically, with this guarded mind and heart, you will feel poor for a moment, and you will also be stunned into an embarrassing silence.

History of Non-Dualism

In the Christian tradition, non-dualism stood the test of time for fifteen hundred years. Certainly *The Cloud of Unknowing*, a Middle English fourteenth-century Christian mystical guide on contemplation, made clear that non-dualism was still very much a part of the Christian tradition, that knowing had to be balanced by unknowing and all saying by not saying. Its underlying message was that the only way to truly know God is to abandon all preconceived notions and beliefs or knowledge about God and surrender to unknowingness, at which point you begin to glimpse the true nature of God. What is sometimes called the apophatic or "darkness" tradition of not knowing had been a central part of Christian teaching since Dionysius in the late sixth century, whom even the Scholastic theologians Aquinas and Bonaventure still made use of extensively in the thirteenth century.

When you put knowing together with not knowing, and even become willing not to know, you have this marvelous phenomenon called faith, which allows you to keep an open horizon, an open field. You can thus remain in a humble and wondrous beginner's mind, even as you grow older, maybe even more so.

Today, scientists seem to do this better than many Christian clergy in this regard. Those in the scientific community can live with a working hypothesis, can move forward with theory, while too many in the religious community cannot; they need to have the whole truth right now and in clear and certain words: "My denomination has the whole truth; your denomination/religion does not." What a waste of time. Can't we see that is largely love of self more than love of truth? We got even more practiced in such a style after the Reformation when Europe divided initially into Catholics and Lutherans. Each group had to prove that it was 100 percent right, and the other group was 100 percent wrong—which was and is, of course, never true.

And then, right on the heels of the Reformation, we had this strangely named phenomenon, the Enlightenment. They stole our word! Did you ever think of that? That was a New Testament concept, largely emerging from Jesus, who said that he was the Enlightener (John 8:12) and that we would share in that enlightenment (John 9; Matthew 5:14–16). How did such a broad and spiritual meaning come to mean being merely rational? We lost our own unique and brilliant way of knowing as we tried to ape our antagonists and borrowed their very limited vocabulary and perspective.

Rationality is a fine mode of thinking. It produced the Industrial Revolution, the Scientific Revolution, the Mechanical Revolution, and the Medical Revolution. Most of us would not be sitting here without it right now. Thank you, God, for the dualistic, rational mind! It is so good as far as it goes, but it cannot go far enough. There is a ceiling above which the rational mind cannot go.

In *The Naked Now*, I suggest that there are five issues above the ceiling that the rational mind can not process or explain:

> *Love*. Love is not rational. We know that, and yet most of us
>   would die for it.
> *Death*. Death itself is not rational, cannot be explained.
> *Life* itself, what a mystery.
> *Suffering*, through which many people break down in the

presence of something they try through ego to resolve
rationally, or dualistically, and try to blame somebody
for it.

Any notion of *infinity* or eternity blows the very sockets of
the mind.

More recently, I have actually added a sixth: *sex.* Anyone who
has had sex would admit that there is nothing rational about it.
And yet people live and die for it.

What made us ever think that the truly great things were
only rational? When we limit understanding these issues to
a mere rational level, we close down being open to the non-
rational, our emotional intelligence, the intuitive, the personal,
and the contextual—all of which are necessary to know something spiritually or fully. We have tried to resolve crucial issues
at that level with dualistic morality, dogmas, and doctrines,
which is low-level consciousness, and cannot get to the higher
levels or to mystical experience.

Today, we are living in a marvelous time, a time when the
contemplative mind is being rediscovered. And the only reason
I said "yes" to the invitation to the Festival of Faiths was
because just down the road from here Thomas Merton almost
single-handedly pulled back the veil and reintroduced the word
contemplation to a Catholic Church that no longer understood it
and to a Protestant era that was never taught the concept at all.
Thank God, there were many exceptions—those people who by
great love and great suffering came to a contemplative mind on
their own, without even knowing they were contemplatives or
ever using the word to describe themselves in that way.

The Church, after the Reformation and after the Enlightenment, circled the wagons into a little defensive shell. We called it a "siege mentality." Each of the other Christian denominations did the same. We each lusted after certitude and order and explanation to prove that our denomination was right, as if that was faith—or love. Not realizing that much of the world would look at us and conclude that our whole religion was wrong, if it could waste time on such egocentric fighting! For the most part, contemplation was no longer systematically taught, even in the religious orders, and even within contemplative communities themselves, as Thomas Merton prophetically told his brothers.

And yet, there are many people whose souls still live in that silent, spacious, open place, and this is invariably the fruit of great love or great suffering and usually both. This is the natural path and universally available path to contemplation for all people. You do not need to be celibate, monastic, or even especially ascetical (except in your mind and heart) to be a contemplative.

Although the universally available paths are love and great suffering, conscious inner prayer will accelerate the path to contemplation and transformation.[9] But the mere reciting of prayers can also be, as St. John Cassian (360–435) called it, a *pax perniciosa*, "dangerous peace." This early Christian monk, who brought the ideas and practices of Egyptian monasticism to the early medieval West, saw that even the way of prayer can be dangerous if it never leads you to great love and allows you to avoid necessary suffering in the name of religion.

What those who fall into the safety net of silence find is that it is not at all a fall into individualism. In fact, if it is, it is that dangerous peace. True prayer or contemplation is instead a leap into commonality and community. You know that what you are experiencing is held by the whole and that you are not alone anymore. You are a part, and forever a grateful part.

That is why you can, if you are called to it, be celibate, because you live a kind of intimacy with everything. Everything is a jolt, a joy, a possibility, a communion, a connection. In fact, celibacy is wrong for anybody to choose if they have not moved to some level of contemplative prayer because basically *it is not going to work*, and they will end up as "fruitless and frustrated bachelors and spinsters" as Pope Francis says. That is also why we have had the pedophilia scandals. Well-intentioned young boys went off to seminaries, thinking they could live life at this deeper level, and did not have the inner tools to know how to do it.

On a lesser level, the Church did the same thing to the laity by telling them to believe doctrines, such as those of the Trinity or the two natures of Christ, neither of which can be understood with a dualistic mind. All you can do is intellectually assent to such doctrines, but they have no dynamic possibility in your soul that opens up your heart or opens up your mind or gives you foundational peace. In fact, they close the heart and mind because you are living in a kind of unreality.

The principle of three, which we call Trinity, undoes the principle of two, and it says that all of the power is in the relationship between. As Cynthia Bourgeault, Canadian theologian, Episcopal priest, writer and retreat leader, says, "Because the whole important thing about the doctrine of the Trinity is all the power is not in the names of the three particles, but in the relationship between."[10]

There is a foundational pattern of giving and receiving in every aspect of the universe—modeled on the very shape of God as Trinity. Once you have a dynamic waterwheel of outflowing love, as Franciscan St. Bonaventure called it, the flow only flows in one direction, always positive, always giving, always outpouring, where there is no possibility of anger, unlove, wrath, or hatred in God.

The doctrine of the Trinity was made to order to move us to the dynamic principle of three, where there is always movement forward. But the ego naturally pulled us back into the principle of two, which is inherently comparative, competitive, and antagonistic, and usually either/or. Trinity undoes that. All you can do is jump into the flow and allow it to happen. And the only way of really jumping in is through standing in love—even in your mind. An aphorism I often use is this: "Watch your thoughts; they become words. Watch your words; they become actions. Watch your actions; they become habits. Watch your habits; they become your character. Watch your character; it becomes your destiny." Contemplation and silence nip the ego and its negatives in the bud by teaching you how to watch and guard your very thoughts.

Solitude Versus Silence

Now I want to make an important distinction between solitude and silence. Solitude, of itself, is not silence. Solitude emerges perhaps because you do not like people, or you are angry at your spouse, or you want to get away from noisy people—or you are just an introvert—and there is nothing inherently wrong or right about that. But there is nothing transformative about this kind of solitude. It is running, the opposite of connecting. A true solitude has to fall into a larger silence, a shared silence, something much beyond the absence of noise. True silence holds the contraries in a way that words cannot. It mediates and resolves the polarities from each side. Silence is the space in between words and around ideas. Each side of every argument must travel over the broad appeasing surface of silence before it can reach the other. And walking over that broad road of silence, one is much more humble and less judgmental about the other side. Silence also does not put words into the mouth of the other or make caricatures of the other side. It certainly does not call names but patiently waits for the other to fully name himself or herself.

Without that silence around words and around ideas, there is only more analysis and endless commentary. This is what we *cease* to do in contemplative practice. We stop the commentary, especially once we realize how self-referential most of the commentary is. Such inner dialogues with ourselves will never get us anywhere close to Great Truth.

We all have rehearsed an upcoming argument in our heads, whether it is with a boss, wife, or husband, or someone close to us. Just like the prodigal son returning home, practicing what he is going to say to Dad. The fearful ego practices its defensive posture.

But when we do that, notice we use the words that are going to win our case, to defeat the other side. We are not, if we are honest with ourselves, really searching for truth, but rather searching to look good, to look right, to keep the job, to keep our marriage, or whatever it might be. And God surely understands that.

But the contemplative mind moves beyond that to read reality at a different level than either/or. We named my last book *Yes, And . . .* rather than *Yes, But* because the "but" makes the phrase contrary—this, not that. It sets us up for antagonistic or defensive thinking.

As a Catholic priest, I am trained in the Tradition; I know the Tradition and I know orthodoxy. But we Franciscans often think of ourselves as a kind of alternative orthodoxy inside the Church, emphasizing different things. In general, Francis emphasized orthopraxy over mere verbal orthodoxy, focusing on how you *live* over what you say you *believe*. We are now seeing the same emphasis in his namesake, Pope Francis, and it is setting the world on fire.

Francis was not an academic. He emphasized living a simple, nonviolent life in this world. The line attributed to him that is popular today is actually a paraphrase of something he says to us in our Franciscan Rule and in one of his "Admonitions": "Preach the gospel at all times. When necessary, use words." He also says similar things to the friars in his earliest biographies.

Preach the gospel at all times. Lifestyle was itself the gospel, the emphasis—similar to the traditions of the Mennonites, Amish, Waldensians, and Quakers. Let's not argue about words because it always leads to dualistic taking of sides. Let's just live in a way that shouts Jesus. Live in a way that no one can deny exudes the love and the compassion of Jesus.

Silence, of course, is not fighting about any doctrine, but agreeing not to fully know, and not to speak too quickly. It is a way of life more than a doctrine that you can impose. Inside of silence—especially extended silence—we see that things find their true order and meaning somewhat naturally. When things find their true order, we know what is important, what lasts, what is real, what Jesus would call the reign of God or the Kingdom of God, or in other words, the big stuff. All the rest is passing. All those things you were emotional about last Wednesday that you cannot even remember are what the Buddhists rightly call emptiness. They have no lasting substance, and in that sense they are not real.

And yet we give our lives for emotions that are over and gone by next week. We wrap our egos around them and give them a weight and importance they do not deserve. Feelings are inherently self-referential, which helps us know ourselves, but also keeps us in our own little world if we take them too seriously or attach to them. Feelings are first of all always about "me," which gives us good self knowledge but also traps us in that very self if we do not use them to go further.

My metaphor for Jesus's Kingdom of God is simply The Big Picture. In The Big Picture, what matters? When you are on your deathbed, what will matter? Will you be thinking about what you are thinking about now? Will you be arguing about what you are arguing about now? To pull back from the tug of emotion and ego that wants to be right, wants to win, wants to put the other down, wants to humiliate the enemy, is the very heart of spiritual warfare. This is where we need to put our energy first, instead of obsessing about theoretical or real moral issues that usually ask little of us personally.

There is something we find so sweet about taking sides,

about feeling we've made our case. But silence allows things to emerge in their wholeness—as Ken Wilber would say, "all levels, all stages"—instead of our usual being trapped at one level, one stage.

At that one level, that one stage, we each make our case. And that is why all arguments between people at different levels of growth are doomed to some degree of misunderstanding. Outside the contemplative mind, those arguments are almost always egocentric and about winning. Our United States Congress has made this overwhelmingly clear in recent years, as otherwise educated representatives can speak so narrowly and blindly, so much so that we now expect it of them. Such a level of conversation is not about the love or the pursuit of truth as such, or even reality. It is about the love of victory, which is pretty much all that the ego wants, along with making sure the other side loses.

The dualistic mind loves to exaggerate the differences, anything that can be considered a defect in the other person. When you have not experienced communion, when you have not experienced unitive consciousness, all you have are your differences. They become an easy reference point, and you choose to overplay them. It is the early stages of what René Girard will rightly call "the scapegoat mechanism," and he says it largely operates unconsciously. Contemplation is about making you conscious of such things!

In the first half of life, we are all rather dualistic and even need to start there. We need to first make distinctions before we can then move beyond them. How can we not? We expect young people to make distinctions and focus upon winning.

They know their group, their team, their nationality, their race, their religion, their neighborhood. Most of history has been in a first-half-of-life consciousness up to now.

Most people never had time for, or modeling of, the second half of life, where it is not about winning anymore, but rather about being and inner integrity. And silence is what makes space for that larger and truer level of being, if we *allow* it!

We need to see silence, and nothingness itself, as a kind of being in the great chain of being, maybe the first link from which all others emerge. St. Bonaventure, the Italian spiritual genius who picked up the intellectual thread from the non-academic Francis, led us through the great chain of being from material things, to inner soul, to the Divine. John Duns Scotus, another early Franciscan, said you may speak of being with one voice from the being of the earth itself, to the waters upon the earth to the minerals within the earth, the flowers and trees and grasses, the animals, the humans, the angelic choirs, the divine. Both of these mystics would have said that once you stop seeing the divine in any one link of that chain, the whole thing will fall apart. It is either all God's work or you have a hard time finding God in mere parts. That split and confused world is the post-modern world we live in today, which no longer knows how to surround and ground all things in silence.

This is not an oversimplification. Either you see God in all things, or very quickly you cannot see God anywhere, even in your own species. And yet we Christians have spent the last five hundred years since the Reformation dividing and deciding where God was, believing God is in *our* church, but not in yours. Interestingly enough, we determined it was usually "my church" that God preferred and where God resided. It was the very lie that Jesus tried to undo among his own chosen people, and he experienced the same backlash.

Even in the *Baltimore Catechism*, which generations of American Catholic young people were raised on, the Church gave mixed messages about God. The answer to the question "Where is God?" (question 16) was "God is everywhere." But then throughout the rest of the catechism, we learned that God really is *not* everywhere, but only in the Roman Catholic Church. And in the Roman Catholic Church, Jesus is only in the tabernacle. And that was only if the priest celebrated a valid Mass and was in the state of grace. And thus God was locked up, and only the priest possessed the key. We unwittingly laid a foundation for modern atheism, because we kept saying where God was *not*, and where God was not even *allowed* to be. Immature Christianity actually gave birth to secularism by not appreciating the silence and the beauty and the grace glue that connects everything with everything else in the universe. We did this by not honoring the humble silence that precedes all our words and distinctions.

What happened was, while claiming on the one hand that God is everywhere, we asserted, in effect, that God is hardly anywhere.

Silence allows the whole, and does not get lost in and over-identify with the parts. Without silence, almost all things become boring, superfluous or just another thing. And we become preoccupied with size, mass, speed, influence, celebrities, and not with meaning or significance in itself. It seems that only poets and mystics now have time for such things as meaning or depth.

22

Silence is that ever-faithful companion, a portal to constantly deeper connection with whatever is in front of you. That which is in front of you does not need to be big or important. It can be a stone. It can be a grasshopper. Anything can convert you once you surround it with this reverent silence that gives it significance, identity, singularity, importance, value, or what Duns Scotus called the "thisness" of everything.

Scotus, building again on Francis's love of animals and creatures—Brother Sun, Sister Moon—said that God does not create genus and species. God only creates *this*: this frog, this moment, this dog. And the fact that this dog is persisting and being in this moment means that God is choosing it and loving it right now or it would fall into oblivion. Wow, that is good! At least I think so.

There is only thisness in good Franciscan philosophy, which is another way of speaking of the mystery of incarnation. It is why so many poets liked John Duns Scotus. Nineteenth-century English poet and Jesuit priest Gerard Manley Hopkins was a Scotist, as was twentieth-century American Trappist monk and mystic Thomas Merton. The Jesuit Teilhard de Chardin would be Scotus's modern counterpart in his love of material and concrete things.

Summary

Silence is a dwelling place that is at once horizontal, allowing connection with the thisness, the singularity of everything, but also, at the same time, vertical. It allows us to find through those things doorways to the eternal. Silence takes away the noise we project onto everything and allows individual things to stand in, stand for, and even stand apart so that we can see the light and life that they reveal. This *is always the doorway to* that—*and to more*. The one is the window by which we can see the many. If it is true here, it soon becomes true everywhere.

Silence attracts meaning. If you stay silent for a whole hour it will be hard not to write a poem.

In silence, everything becomes real. Everything deserves a poem. Silence discloses the fullness of the now, instead of always waiting and wanting more, instead of waiting for the next thing, the more exciting thing, to happen.

But what we have to remember is *how we do anything is how we do everything*. And how we do this moment is how we are going to do the next moment. And if we're bored to death with this moment, we're going to be bored to death with the next moment.

We have to be awake right now. And we can be through silence. It is not a matter of being more moral but of being more conscious—which will eventually make you much more moral! What it means to be vulnerable before a moment is to give it the power to change us. If we do not give another person, another animal, event, situation, or emotion the power to influence us, to change us, then we are not intimate with the moment, not vulnerable before the only reality we have.

In many ways, intimacy before the moment, vulnerability in the presence of all reality, is the very name of spirituality. It would be indeed heroic if we could live our whole life inside of this kind of semi-permeable membrane. It would allow all events in, enough to really change us, and allow us out of our prisons—to change the world a bit, I would hope. If our spirituality does not make us more vulnerable, I doubt whether it is much good.

Silence, if you respond to a little bit of it, sort of hides. But if you remain open, then it reveals more. It reveals and hides, it reveals and hides, it reveals and hides. It waits and sees if you are going to use it in a non-manipulative way, and if you remain non-manipulative, it gives even more of itself. Please think about that for a while.

So be patient with silence. It gives a little, and then it gives more if you do not abuse the first little. It is like floating in water; once you stop fighting it, you float even better.

Leave the silence open-ended. Do not try to settle the dust. Do not rush to resolve the inner conflict. Do not seek a glib, quick answer, but leave all things for a while in the silent space. Do not rush to judgment. That is what it really means that God alone is the judge. Inner silence frees you from the burden of thinking that your judgment is needed or important.

Real silence moves you from knowing things to perceiving a presence that has a reality in itself. Could that be God? There is then a mutuality between you and all things. There is an I-thou relationship, as twentieth-century philosopher Martin Buber would call it. He said an I-it relationship is when we experience everything as a commodity, as useful, as utilitarian. But the I-thou relationship is when you can simply respect a thing as it is without adjusting it, naming it, changing it, fixing it, controlling it, or trying to explain it. Is that the mind that can know God? I really think so.

Such silence is the peace the world cannot give (John 14:27). Now that does not mean that there is not a place for explaining, not a place for understanding. But you first have to learn to say "yes" to the moment. Yes is where you have to begin. If you start with no, which is critiquing, judging, pigeonholing, analyzing, dismissing, it is very hard to get back to yes.

You must learn to start every single encounter with a foundational yes, before you ever dare to move to no. That is the heart of contemplation, and it takes a lifetime of practice. But you have now begun and can live each day with a forever-returning beginner's mind. It will always be silent before it dares to speak.

Two

Sacred Silence, Pathway to Compassion

God as Flow

It is strange to me that Christianity, the religion that believes the Word became flesh, has become so wordy that much of its history has become fighting about words, using words in different ways, defining words, defending words. We reversed the incarnational process of God, and made the flesh become word again (but no longer the Eternal Word!).

You would think that we would have been much more concerned for what we call incarnation, the enfleshment, the physical world, if we believed what we said we believe: that God became incarnate in this Jewish man called Jesus. That is the belief of the Christian tradition. But our history has been quite Gnostic if we are honest, more like *excarnation* than incarnation, invariably preferring theory over practice.

Something supremely orthodox in the Christian tradition is the doctrine of the Trinity. The shape of God in orthodox Christian belief is that God is more a verb than a noun. God is a relationship. God is a communion between those we call Father, Son, and Holy Spirit. We gave them masculine names, although we always argue about whether the Holy Spirit is feminine.

But as theologian Cynthia Bourgeault says, even in that composition, women still lose: There is the Father and the Son, and it is still two to one. She urges us not to argue about whether the figures of the Trinity are all masculine or all feminine, as it misses the point. The important thing to focus on is *the relationship*, not the precise names or gender of the three persons.

What happened is that we pulled what we believed was the Incarnate One, the Visible One, the Christ, out of this process of communion, of mutual outpouring, which words prove inadequate to describe and which cannot be talked about. The doctrine of the Trinity could have given us much more patience with silence and mystery. But we wanted something to talk about. So the Visible One, Christ Jesus, became the One we mostly talked about. We pretty much treated Jesus as God, and forgot that the Trinity was God, which significantly rearranged the Christian mind, and made mysticism much more rare and even mistrusted.

To put it very honestly, we Christians overplayed the Jesus card. We pulled Jesus out of this dynamic union of the Trinity, and then we pushed Jesus, for all practical purposes into the God role, when his role was much different—*it was to put God and humanity into one*! We did not know how to put it together in him, and the sad result was that we had no model or suggestion that we could also put the two together in ourselves.

Let us look at our first attempts at language to describe the indescribable, though we might use different vocabulary today. Our use of masculine words is, at least in part, a historical accident, with the use of the word *Father* to describe God as the Creator and Source. Jesus himself described his God as

Abba, Father—actually "Daddy"—and this was very helpful in a world where the male was usually patriarchal and mistrusted and surely not a loving daddy. Jesus calling God Abba began the needed healing, but unfortunately we took the metaphor literally, and it created a lot of push back and negative projection over time. God the Father ended up looking like another patriarch instead of letting the Trinitarian flow redefine the very notion of patriarchy itself (which I hope will become clear), or learning to relate to this Father the way that Jesus did.

We say the doctrine of the Trinity is the absolute foundational theology of Christianity. Yet German Jesuit Karl Rahner said back in the early 1960s, "Should the doctrine of the Trinity have to be dropped as false, the major part of religious literature could well remain virtually unchanged."[11] How could this be true? It is not bad will or even bad theology, but we simply lacked the inner tools to deal with it. The doctrine of the Trinity invites and, in fact, necessitates, non-dual consciousness, a contemplative mind to even begin to process this non-rational mystery of God.

Other religions do not have to accept the Christian vocabulary and the Christian metaphor of the Trinity. But while we use different language, most religions at the mature levels have come to a notion of God as a dynamic flow, a communion, God as relationship itself, or the very "Ground of Being" as Paul says (Acts 17:28).

This Father God was the God that our Jewish ancestors had discovered and reverenced that was first of all beyond words, whose name—Yahweh—could not be spoken (Exodus 3:14 and 20:7). In fact, that is why they did not use the sacred name. It was unspeakable, and our Jewish ancestors gave us a marvelous sense of humility before God and Yahweh's ineffability. To use this name was to use it "in vain." "You do not know what you are talking about when you use the word, God"[12] was the eternal message. Any word is in vain, and yet some word must be spoken.

With the use of the wonderful metaphor "Father" (remember that nothing else is possible but metaphors for God), Christian belief of the Formless One took form because we humans had to picture one whom we could love and to whom we could relate (1 John 1:1–2). We had to start with a healing metaphor to begin a trustful relationship, but the trouble is that we took the metaphor literally and thought that God was actually of the human male gender. Rather silly when you think of it, but at least it was a start.

The one Christians call the Holy Spirit was precisely the love relationship between Father and Son, which again could not be named, and never perfectly described. S/he is the "Third Something" that takes on a reality and life of its own, like the love relationship between a husband and wife. The best we could do was come up with further metaphors, like descending dove, fire, wind, flowing water—all dynamic words and helpful symbols to describe the active and living relationship, the inner movements, that we call the Indwelling Holy Spirit.

We forget too often that *the only possible language of religion is metaphor.* It comes as a great shock to most Christians that every word we use is metaphorical: it is like, it is like, it is like. If we as a Christian community would have been more honest and accepted the Jewish commandment that any name for God is in vain and is not a perfect or adequate description, we would have developed much more humility around words—and around religion itself. Even now, many Catholics look for mystery through incense and Latin instead of resting in and struggling with the foundational mystery itself.

We were called to honor the Father and the Holy Spirit and the one who took shape and identity, and the relationship between them, instead of just focusing on Jesus, which became the Christian religion in its most common forms. And it is that overemphasis on Jesus and less on relationship which also had the consequence of setting us in competition with the other world religions. We have to prove Jesus all the time, and in contradistinction to Buddha, Allah, Hindu gods, or even the God of Israel. In doing so, we pulled the Christ out of the very union that he talked about, that he enjoyed, and invited us into. An honest Trinitarianism actually opens up interfaith dialogue and respect, because now we can admit that God is also total mystery and inner aliveness, and not Jesus apart from these.

That is the irony of it—we ended up not being faithful to our own tradition by overemphasizing merely one part of it. We prayed *to* Christ instead of as the official prayers still say "*through* Christ our Lord." We forgot the shape of God and how we were a part of that shape as the "body of Christ." What an enormous loss.

When we overplayed the Jesus card and made Jesus into the founder of our new religion, we forgot that he died, I believe, a faithful Jew. He did not know he was founding the Christian religion in his human mind (which is rather clear from the Gospels, if we are honest about them); but he was trying to reform his own—and all religion—from its idolatries. I surely hope Catholics know that he never heard of the Roman Catholic Church, or any other church for that matter. He went to the synagogue and temple. Shocking for us, I suppose, but a necessary shock.

The Tangent of History

We have to recognize that we understood our Christian religion outside of any honest historical context. What happened very soon was that we not only separated from our roots in Judaism, but we then aligned ourselves with the Roman Empire after AD 313 and aligned with power and war and money in Europe, largely until the second half of the twentieth century when the two world wars revealed the whole mismatch for all of the world to see.

While that confluence of events had some good aspects—I am not saying they are all bad—our alignment with the Roman Empire, the Holy Roman Empire, the Spanish Monarchy, and the English empire made it again and again necessary to defend and to prove our God was better than other gods. Empires need an agreed upon god to hold together, and it does not matter if we actually follow his teachings. This humble Jewish man—Jesus—becomes a theocratic figure. The Incarnate one became the Transcendent Judge again. He becomes the Pantocrator (Omnipotent and Wrathful Lord of the Universe) with almost no basis in Scripture. Compare that to the simple drawings of the Good Shepherd and the "Crucified Ass" that we find in the catacombs. These Byzantine drawings are entirely different images of Jesus that profoundly influenced and continue to influence Christian practice to this day.

The very Latin word for God—*Deus*—is really a form of the Greek word *Zeus*. We were basically dealing with a pagan notion of god, and this became Jesus, who soon had hardly anything to do with the historical Jesus anymore, but he was the available and needed God figure that held the whole Roman Empire together. In fact, some art historians teach that the Pantocrator image which took over Christian basilicas after the fourth century is a precise attempt to imitate the foreboding image of Zeus (Jove or Jupiter) in his Greek and Roman temples. A crucified loser Jesus was not an image with which an empire or the ego was comfortable. Or ever will be.

There were always people who went to the deeper level, what I call the underground stream, where the unspeakable, the mystery, was still honored and allowed. But by and large, we moved from our position as the immoral minority to the seeming moral majority, and that radically shifted our vantage point.

The deeper and older stream can be found, of course, in John's Gospel and many of Paul's teachings, later in the Desert Fathers and Mothers, and soon moving into Egypt, Syria, Cappadocia in eastern Turkey, and areas of Palestine. This is where the mystical tradition first developed, where the contemplative life was discovered and taught, revealing that we needed a different mind to comprehend such high-level teaching. They did not fight about doctrines, but instead about the best ways to find *inner quiet*! Try to feel the radical difference that makes. Read *The Philokalia*, a collection of fourth- through fifteenth-century texts from the Eastern Orthodox Church, if you want to know this for yourself.

They were able to demonstrate and teach that the normal,

early-stage dualistic mind cannot get you to "understand spiritual things in a spiritual way" (1 Corinthians 2:13). It is too weak an instrument to understand what it might mean when Jesus says "the Father and I are one," and that we are actually sharing with you this same Spirit, and inviting you into our relationship.

You cannot understand this new principle of three with the old principle of two, of dualism, which is always antagonistic, either/or, right-or-wrong kind of thinking. This dualistic thinking continued in Roman Catholicism throughout the centuries and did much to create the two-level Christianity (clerics/religious versus laity) that Luther rightly reacted against.

Monks and friars and nuns, while not all contemplatives, formed the heart of every religious community (like my own Franciscan community) and were responsible for the rediscovery of the contemplative mind in our time—the Kentucky monk, Thomas Merton, led the charge into the past and back into our future. So many early religious became hermits because they could not survive in the common dualistic religious life. Many lay people, through great love and great suffering, became "hidden contemplatives," but usually with little support from the clergy, so they also stepped to the side to survive.

Whenever you see a recurrence of hermits, anchorites, recluses, and hermitages, you can know that such an age has rediscovered non-dual or contemplative thinking. You cannot endure silence and solitude for long with a dualistic mind. You drive yourself crazy with your inner arguments.

Unfortunately, however, this splitting off did create a two-level society, and the normal Catholic in the normal Church in

Florence or Heidelberg or Boston really was not expected to learn the contemplative mind. He or she was just taught to pay, pray, and obey. The praying did not really mean contemplative prayer, but rather the saying of prayers, or the social prayer of liturgy, where you can know if you are doing it right or wrong, which is a strong ego need. Unfortunately, there is little call to honest shadow work, humility, or mystery at this level. It is mostly about conforming to the group.

The marvel of living in our time is that this tradition of contemplation is being retrieved and named honestly again. Yes, we had it, we lost it, but we continually rediscover it. Up to now it has been marginalized, somewhere off to the edge so that it was not expected from or offered to the ordinary Christian believer— or the ordinary clergy who did all the preaching and teaching. That is fundamentally why Catholicism split into at least three major levels: the clergy who held it all together, the laity who did what the clergy told them to do, and the monks, nuns, and friars who, in effect, moved off to the side to find the old depth—with varying degrees of success, of course.

Then, thank God for the Protestant Reformation in the sixteenth century, because, up to that point, we Catholics were the only game in town; we had a monopoly on supposed Christianity, at least in the West. There was no loyal opposition to keep Christianity somewhat on target, or even honest, especially since we had lost almost all contact with the Eastern Church after the Great Schism of 1054. We learned again and again that absolute power tends to corrupt absolutely.

Without prophetic thinking, that is, self-critical thinking, which we originally learned from the Jews, all religion becomes idolatrous and self-serving. The Reformation tried to reform, but it was not largely a recovery of the contemplative tradition. Instead, Christianity became even more heady, more verbal, more argumentative than it had been before. And, of course, this was accompanied by the invention of the printing press, which had the side effect of moving us largely into the left brain with both good and bad forms of rational thinking. It had to happen. We had to go through it.

But now we are at the end of five centuries of endless Christian argumentation which the world is just tired of and does not listen to anymore. The historical issues over which we divided are not even interesting to most people inside or outside. It is surely hard for outsiders to take us seriously, since each group claims it is the only one that Jesus loves and is following him correctly, and we reveal little of the mystical, dynamic, Trinitarian flow of life and life between us, within us, or toward others.

Naturally and rightfully, we Christians find ourselves in a very defensive position today because the secular West says, "Show us the fruit, show us the future." Where did the two world wars come from? They did not come from pagan Asia, as we thought of it, but the little continent that we Christians thought we had in the bag. We were all Catholics and Christians in that little part of the world called Europe, and that is where world wars happened. That is where the Holocaust happened and where a continent formed by the Christian tradition slaughtered one another twice in one century, and whose preferences and colonies are perhaps the most materialistic in the world to this day. "What happened to Jesus as their ideal and teacher?" the world must be asking.

The irony of the centuries of anti-Semitism in most parts of Europe that laid the ground for the Holocaust was that it was like killing our grandfather. When we separate from our grandparents—which is our Jewish heritage—and we do not even know that that is our grandfather, we end up killing the very ones we should honor and love. It is cultural schizophrenia, and it will stand forever as a massive judgment on the immaturity of Western Christianity and our amazing capacity for missing the point. It is also a final bad fruit of dualistic thinking—which insists on an enemy, a scapegoat onto whom we can dump our own untransformed evil.

When we lose the contemplative mind, or non-dual consciousness, we invariably create violent people. The dualistic mind is endlessly argumentative, and we created an argumentative continent, which we also exported to North and South America. We see it in our politics; we see it in our Church's inability to create any sincere interfaith dialogue—or even intra-faith dialogue. The Baptists are still fighting the Anglicans as "lost" and the Evangelicals are dismissing the Catholics as the "Whore of Babylon," and we Catholics are demeaning everybody else as heretics, and each of us is hiding in our small, smug circles. What a waste of time and good God-energy, while the world suffers and declines. We have divided Jesus.

Simone Weil, that marvelous French philosopher and political activist stood on the edge of Christianity and Judaism her whole life, wanting her very life to be a bridge—loving both of them and not being able to choose either of them. Her great message was that the trouble with Christianity is that it had made itself into a separate religion instead of recognizing that the prophetic message of Jesus might just be necessary for the reform and authenticity of all religions.

But Christians made Christianity into a competition, and once we were in competition, we had to be largely verbal; soon we were aggressive and, saddest of all, we became quite violent—all in the name of God. But, one follows from the other, and unless you nip it in the bud of thoughts and feelings—which is what contemplative prayer does—your thoughts invariably become words, your words become actions, your actions become habits, your habits become your character, and your character becomes your final destiny.

Yet I cannot doubt and deny, because I was lucky enough to be exposed to it as a Franciscan, that the deeper stream was always there, the stream of contemplation. It was never the mainstream, and we have to be honest about that now. It was relegated to a minority position. And even today, when you tell most Christians about contemplation, it can sound heretical, new, or unnecessary.

When you know the Tradition (with the big T), the Judeo-Christian perennial tradition, and you discover the deeper stream, it is just so easy to communicate with brothers and sisters of other faith traditions. We can talk from a common base. I was trained in Catholic orthodox traditional theology, and that very Judeo-Christian tradition, at the contemplative level, taught me to honor the visibility and revelation of God in all the world traditions. What a paradox, but not really at all. When you go deep in one place, you invariably fall into the deep and common underground stream.

Our Living School in Albuquerque, New Mexico, is trying to

reintroduce the West to what we call the Perennial Tradition, the underground stream that we all share. That does not mean I encourage you to abandon your own mother tradition. You have to know the rules before you can know how to break the rules properly. You have to be surrendered and accountable to one Tradition, as even the Dalai Lama and Mother Teresa both insisted. Otherwise, your ego self is always the decider, and you operate outside the living Body of Christ.

In that deeper and underground stream, silence is much more possible because we know that all words are inadequate anyway; all words are faulty, all words are "yes, and." I think if we could surround our religions with that kind of humility, with that kind of patience, we all would find this conversation entirely easy and natural.

Responses to Father Rohr from representatives of other faiths:

Rajiv Mehrotra, *an independent filmmaker and producer, is the managing trustee of the Public Service Broadcasting Trust and chairman of The Media Foundation, and serves as the secretary and founding trustee of the Foundation for Universal Responsibility of His Holiness the Dalai Lama.*

I cannot help but feel, Father Richard, that you are unduly harsh on your faith. As I mentioned before the break, I think that when we look at all traditions, the metaphysical aspiration is essentially a fringe aspiration of all traditions.

Turning to His Holiness (the Dalai Lama), he has had deep admiration for the Christian tradition and particularly for the tradition of service, of compassion, of reaching out to help people, and he so often talks about how that is something that Tibetan monks and monasteries should look out for and learn from.

Having said that, when I rushed to the restaurant after the break, I overhead a conversation: "Why don't they talk about prayer? Why don't they talk about action, manifesting compassion in action?" I think that those in the Eastern traditions have fought hard about different mental dispositions and how the pursuit of action and moving away from mysticism affected your mental disposition and your proclivity. It is called *karma yoga*—you perform dispassionate actions, distancing yourself from the fruits of action—that enables you to perform right action. His Holiness, in Tibetan vocabulary, would talk about motivation, the importance of motivation in the actions that you perform.

You spoke about God and the value of relationships, the value of community in being able to nurture silence, and I think the rabbi (Arthur Green) could perhaps talk about the notion of the Sabbath, of a community silence. In Buddhism we have the great importance of the Sun God having a community that enables and empowers the cultivation of silence. Would you share that with us?

Rabbi Arthur Green, rector of Hebrew College's Rabbinical School. We have all much to learn from one another, and those of us in the Jewish tradition who respect the contemplative aspect of our tradition and the mystical aspect are very grateful to the Catholic Church for having preserved so much of that mystical tradition for many, many years.

God is a verb. The Hebrew name for God, which I still do not pronounce but which is transcribed in English as YHWH—if I had my blackboard here I would show you—is an impossible compilation of the verb "to be." *Haya* is past and *hove* is the present and *Yihiye* is the future. If you take past, present, and future all together and put them in a firm form that does not exist, you get YHWH, the name of God. It really should be translated not G-o-d but "Is was will be." "Is was will be" all at once. You cannot say that, of course, so we substitute for it . . . It is too holy to be spoken by mere mortals like us.

When Moses goes down into Egypt, God reveals the name to him and then [Moses] says, "If the people ask me what do you call 'What you say'? and God says, "I am that I am" or "I shall be what I shall be," which means "I am really a verb. Here is my name. But if you think that name is a noun, which is to say, if you can put me in a little box and say, 'I have God,' I will be what I will be. I will go conjugate myself and become a verb again. I will fly away and be a verb again. I will be a verb, which is to say, I am the one you cannot catch; I am the ultimately inaccessible one."

Of course, Trinitarianism is not our problem, it is not our language.

I think that is the conversation we in some ways should be having, the East/West conversation. What is the meeting point between our Western monotheism and the monism that underlies so much of Eastern religion that you and I seem to know and we all seem to know is there in our contemplative traditions as well? How do we build the bridge between a monotheistic language, which we at this end of the table—Westerners— have inherited, and the truth that we know lies behind it, the truth that there is only one?

That is part of what should be on our table and it has something to do with the vagaries of violence and competition, because as long as there is only one God, that it is my God and not yours, when there is only one, there is not much room to talk about it anymore.

Seyyed Hossein Nasr, professor of Islamic Studies at George Washington University in Washington, D.C.

I want to come back to two comments on something, which is crucial for the understanding between various religions. One is that God is a verb, and one is that the Trinity is a supreme reality. I speak here as both a humble student of religion and as a Muslim who knows a little bit about Islamic thought.

A verb is always in time. A verb implies time. To say that God is a verb is to temporalize God. God cannot be a verb in the ordinary sense. In the same way that God can be referred to as every pronoun, as I, as Thou, as he/she and so forth and so on. The same way God transcends all parts of speech and includes all parts of speech. He cannot be reduced to one part of speech; that is metaphysically absurd.

Secondly, Trinitarianism or Trinity implies relationality. Relationality implies relativity. If God is only relation, then he is no longer absolute. An absoluteness is taken away from the Divine Principle, something which no Hindu metaphysical Shankarananda would ever accept.

Talking from my own tradition, God cannot be relative. Absolute cannot be relative. If there is not absolute, then relativity itself should start meaning a relation to something beyond itself.

So these very profound comments that Richard Rohr made, and I understand where he is coming from, the Franciscan Father, are very important comments. A lot of Christian theologians will now talk about God being relation. But if it is only relation, the statis, God as being, is denied. There one no longer has the metaphysics to speak in a serious manner about the divinity and relation to us.

Certainly Islamic tradition in all of the different schools—Sufi and philosophical schools—stands against this thesis, while understanding that God is always life, so there is divine life. Within divinity that is what it is alluding to, there is divine life. The words *Al-Hai* and *Al-Muhyi,* that is, life and the giver of life, are two divine names mentioned in the Quran.

I, as a humble commentator of what was said, would add these comments and hope one day, of course, with a big audience like this to get into the more important and profound theological issues of what changing our description of divinity from male to female or from noun to verb implies actually for our faith systems.

Three

The True Self Is Compassion, Love Itself

For Christians who have gone to their own depths, which is not all of them I am afraid, there is the uncovering of an Indwelling Presence, which might even be experienced as what Martin Buber calls an "I-thou" relationship. It is a deep and loving "yes" that is inherent within you. In Christian theology, this inner Presence would be described as the Holy Spirit, which is precisely God as immanent, within, and even our deepest and truest self.

Some saints and mystics have described this Presence as "closer to me than I am to myself" or "more me than I am myself." Many of us would also describe this, as Thomas Merton did, as the True Self. Yet, it still must be awakened and chosen. The Holy Spirit is totally given and given equally to all; but it must be received, too. One who totally receives this Presence and draws life from it is what we call a saint.

That is how "image" becomes "likeness," to use the famous two words in the creation of humans (Genesis 1:26–27). We all have the indwelling image, but we surrender to the likeness in varying degrees and stages. None of us are morally or psychologically perfect or whole (at least I have not met any), but a saint or mystic nevertheless dares to believe that he or she is ontologically ("in their very being") whole, and that it is totally a gift from God. It has nothing to do with "me"!

The Holy Spirit is never created by our actions or behavior, but it is naturally indwelling, our inner being with God. In Catholic theology, we called the Holy Spirit "Uncreated Grace." Culture and even religion often teach us to live out of our false self of reputation, self-image, role, possessions, money, appearance, and so on. It is only as this fails us, and it always eventually does, that the True Self stands revealed and ready to guide us, although some enlightened souls surrender to this truth and presence much earlier.

The True Self does not teach us compassion as much as it is compassion already. And from this more spacious and grounded place, one naturally connects, empathizes, forgives, and loves just about everything. We were made in love, for love, and unto love. (This even has scientific and biological evidence today, as we see that our neo-mammalian brain holds positive emotions of *contentment and desire to nurture.* You can see it operating naturally in all mammals as they live in their role peacefully, feed and protect their young, and seem to accept the inevitability of suffering and death much more naturally than we do with our fancy neo-cortex—which wants to fix and explain everything.)

This deep inner "yes" is God in me, is already loving God through me. The false self does not really know how to love, in a very deep or broad way. It is too opportunistic. It is too small. It is too self-referential to be compassionate.

The True Self—where you and God are one—does not choose to love as much as it is love itself already (see Colossians 3:3–4).

Loving from this vast space is experienced as a river within you that flows of its own accord (see John 7:38–39).

Four

Looking Out in Prayer with Contemplative Eyes

To speak of mysticism in simple terms means we speak of *experiential* knowledge of God instead of merely mental or cognitive knowledge of God. And when you really experience the divine, you naturally move to a higher (or deeper) level of consciousness. When most people hear the word *mystical*, they think it means something impossible for most of us or only available to those who are ascetical for twenty-five years. However, mystical encounters come to people who are still weak and sinful, as Jesus makes very clear in many of his stories (the prodigal son, the woman "who was a sinner," and the publican and the Pharisee stories, for example).

A mystical or unitive moment is not something that can be accessed by the left brain, but by the whole brain—right and left—and the heart and the body and the soul together. It is an intuitive *grasp of the whole and by the whole*! That is what makes it so convicting and transformative.

God is another word for the heart of everything and for everything precisely in its connectedness. When you say you love God, you are saying you love everything. Immature religion becomes an excuse for not loving a whole bunch of things and reveals that you have not had an authentic God experience yet. Rigid religion and compulsive religiosity, all unloving religion, is a rather clear sign that you have *not* met God! Once you have had a unitive experience with God, reality, or even yourself, your life invariably shows two things: quiet confidence and joyous gratitude.

That's why mystics can love their enemies, can love the foreigner, can love the outsider. They don't make these distinctions that low-level religion does. Low-level religion is more tribal, a social construct to hold an individual group together. Some believe "I'm Catholic because I'm Irish" or "I'm Catholic because I'm Italian." This is just group identification, and not even close to mystical experience, and, in fact, this often becomes an avoidance of it, as Jesus says to his own Jewish compatriots who tried to claim superiority because they were "sons of Abraham" (Luke 3:8). He even seems to say that the stones beneath his feet could be more fruitful than such futile reliance upon group or blood affiliation (Matthew 3:9).

Organized Religion and the Mystical Path

Organized religion is an example of incarnation. You have to start with the particular to go to the universal. You have to start with the concrete. And, in fact, you need a holding tank, a container to hold you in one spot long enough to learn what the real questions are and to struggle with them. And that's what organized religion does for you. Some form of religion is almost necessary to carry on the Big Tradition, to give you at least the right words to tell you that mystical experience is even desirable or in any way possible. Otherwise, you have to start from zero and go in all ridiculous directions, as often happens in our time.

Organized religion is an accountability system that holds your feet to the fire long enough to know what the issues really are, who God might just be, and what your own limitations might also be.

So, in my vocabulary (and that's all it is) organized religion is very good and almost entirely necessary for what I call the first half of life.[13]

Now, the trouble is that organized religion usually tells you that mystical union with God is possible, but just don't really expect it! That's only for special people. This ends up making mystical moments something very elitist and distant and only available now and then and to a few.

Organized religion often becomes problematic—not wrong, I'm just saying problematic—when you move into the second half of life because it tends, in most instances, not to answer the questions that the soul is asking. Many people have found various forms of parachurch, like the Franciscans. But not everybody is called to be a priest or a nun or even to the Franciscan Third Order. You need to find some way to learn or study or to pray alongside your Sunday worship community, some form of parachurch grouping, which some today call the "emerging church."[14] The Sunday service alone seldom leads people on deeper or even real journeys; we must begin to be honest about this.

All that organized religion can do is to hold you inside the boxing ring long enough so you can begin to ask good questions and expect bigger answers. But it seldom teaches you how to really box with the mystery itself. Organized religion does not tend to cook you! It just keeps you on a low, half-cold simmer. It doesn't teach you how to expect the mystery to show itself at any profound level. It tends, and I don't mean to be unkind, to make you codependent upon its own ministry, instead of leading *you to know something for yourself*, which is really the whole point.

It's like we keep saying, "keep coming back, keep coming back" and you'll eventually get it. But you don't because the whole thing is oriented toward something you attend or watch and not to something you can participate in 24/7, even without the ministrations of priest and ministers and formal sacraments. Again, I mean no disrespect. If God-experience depends on formal sacramental ministry from ordained clergy, then 99.9 percent of creation has had no chance to know or love God. That can't be true.

And if the clergy themselves have not gone on a further journey, they don't know how to send you there or guide you there because they have not gone there themselves yet (see Matthew 23:13). *Nemo dat quod not hat*, we said in Latin: "You cannot give away what you do not have yourself."

The Mystical Path and Daily Life

Father Karl Rahner speaks of "the mysticism of daily life." It's a good phrase. We've got to stop making mysticism something that happens only to celibates and ascetics and monastics.

That's precisely what Francis came to undo in order to bring religious life back to the streets and to the laity and the normal parish, who have always been made to feel like third-class citizens of the kingdom.

You do need to be given a new operating system. I don't care what you are doing. You cannot approach that daily work, that daily job, your family with what I call the dualistic mind, the judgmental, comparative, competitive mind, which most of us are entirely trained in—so much so that we think it is the only mind.[15]

Jesus refers to this as the judgmental mind. That's why He says: "Do not judge" (Matthew 7:1). Maybe we would simply say "Do not label" things. It is just a way of trying to take control and often a game of superiority. The judgmental mind tries to know everything by merely comparing it to something else, which is to start with a negative first step. It is far removed from knowing things in themselves, by themselves, and for themselves. Such low-level attempts at knowing will never get you anywhere close to mystical experience. That's the simplest way to say why the great spiritual teachers always have some form of "Do not judge." The judgmental mind is all too self-referential and closes down the open horizon right away.

The original word for this different mind, this alternative consciousness, and that's what it is, was simply *prayer*. That word has been so misused and trivialized to mean merely petitionary prayer, reading prayers, social prayer (liturgy), or reciting prayers. I'm afraid we Catholics are even known for that: learning formulas and reciting formulas. Many of us had to stop using the word *prayer* and instead use the word *contemplation* so others know we are talking about something different.

I'm not saying that formulaic prayer is wrong, but that is not what was taught by the Desert Fathers and Mothers in the first three or four hundred years of Christianity. That's not the original meaning of prayer. We see this from Jesus's many and long forays into the desert alone, and that the disciples had to coax him to teach them what we call the Our Father (Luke 11:2). Temple prayer or social prayer is not what Jesus is known for, although he surely would not have opposed it unless it became too ritualistic, legalistic, or transactional, as we see when he cleanses the temple. The Gospel does say Jesus and the disciples "sang psalms together" (Mark 14:26; Matthew 26:30), the *Hallel* or Psalms 113–118 which opened and closed the Passover Meal.

Prayer is looking out from a different set of eyes, which are not comparing, competing, judging, labeling, or analyzing, but receiving the moment in its present wholeness and unwholeness. That's what I mean by contemplation. It takes years of practice to switch from our normally dualistic thinking to allow non-dual, receptive prayer to become our primary mode of consciousness.

For many, prayer still means reciting Our Fathers and Hail Marys, and I'm not trying to put down such prayers, especially when they are the *spoken fruit of deeper prayer*. But I know Catholics that have said Our Fathers and Hail Marys all their lives, priests who have said Mass all their lives, and do not know how to pray. That is not a judgment on them, because no one taught them any differently. It is more a deep sadness, because I know without access to the deeper stream, their lives, their celibacy, their ministry will be more about function than unction, to quote Pope Francis's words to a recent clergy gathering.

The goal of prayer, as any good Christian would agree, is to give you access to God and to allow you to listen to God and to actually hear God, if that does not seem presumptuous. But mostly, prayer is to allow you to experience the Indwelling

Presence yourself. You are finally not praying, but prayer is happening through you (see Romans 8:26–27), and you are just the allower and enjoyer.

The only way you can do that is to work to maintain an open field, and, yes, it is work to remain open to grace. What a total paradox. However, it does not mean that grace cannot break through anytime and anywhere. In fact, that is the most common pattern. But we want to enjoy the fruits of grace 24/7 and not just now and then.

If you lead off with the left brain, if you lead off with the judging, calculating, dualistic mind, you will not access the Holy because the only thing that gets in is what you already think, what you already agree with, and what does not threaten you. And God is, by definition, *unfamiliar*, always mysterious, beyond, and more. So if you aren't ready for more and mystery, how can you possibly be ready for God? Your intake valve will be very tight and guarded.

Contemplation is non-dual thinking; it emerges when you don't split the field of the moment between what you already know and what you don't already know as if it is totally wrong or heresy or evil or sinful. I am afraid dualistic thinking is the common mode of thinking, and, of course, the evidence for that is just about everywhere, especially in religion and politics, which is why we cannot meaningfully talk in those split fields.

Can We Trivialize Prayer?

If a whole lot of people are praying for the same thing and apparently at the same time, then there is a tendency to think that prayer is going to bend the arm of God. "More is always better" is the operative assumption here. At this point, I'm not really loving or serving God; I'm trying to get God to be on my side and give me what I want. It necessitates neither love nor surrender, but it is just well-disguised desire to be in control, very often. The wonderful news is, of course, that God is already on my side, so such thinking is futile and a waste of time. It is another way to try to manipulate mystery, as if we could.

There is something compassionate about asking God to heal your grandmother—of course, that's beautiful. But it is still you in the driver's seat trying to get God in your car as a passenger, when God alone can be trusted with the driving. So first you must listen for God's possible will, and not yours, and then, and only then, can you pray in the Spirit.

Jesus warns us about this verbal prayer when he says. "Why do you babble on like the pagans do? God already knows what you need" (Matthew 6:7). He also warns us against telling God what God already knows better than we do (6:9), and I must say many times the formal prayers of the faithful at a Catholic Mass sound more like announcements than actual prayer, especially given the fact that they are done in the third person and not addressed actively as if God is in the room, which would lead us to pray in the second person. (You have to go to Pentecostal or black churches to hear that!) And in that same Gospel, Jesus even warns us against too much public prayer (6:5), since it has too many social payoffs. We must be honest and admit that we have not followed Jesus's basic advice on prayer, and, in fact, often directly disobeyed it.

Jesus does tell us to ask God for what we want (Matthew 7:7-11). He does seem to affirm what we call petitionary or intercessory prayer. Why did Jesus say such a thing? Not to talk God into what we want. Not to announce it to God since God knows and cares about suffering more than we do.

I believe intercessory prayer is important because we need to hear our own thoughts and words out loud. We need to jump on board with what we hope is the will of God and what may well be the will of God. It is an exercise in participation, in unitive caring together with God, what Paul calls divine and human cooperation (Romans 8:28). God does not need our prayers as much as *we need to say them* to even know the deepest will and desire of God—*and our own*. Our prayers are simply seconding the motion.

The first motion is always from God's Spirit working in the soul, making you care about human suffering and need. So when you pray sincerely, God has already spoken to you, and you are just saying "yes" to what God wants even more than you do. That is why prayer leads you to fall in love with God, because you know you are not doing this good thing. It is being done unto you and through you.

It also seems that we don't know our own needs, feelings, thoughts until we speak them. So we all must keep praying "with groans unutterable" (Romans 8:23) until our prayers match the much deeper caring of God, and we discover our own will and God's will are finally the same.

Is Happiness on the Path of Mysticism?

Here is an image that many have offered before me. You don't catch a butterfly by chasing it. You sit still, and the butterfly alights on your shoulder. You don't find happiness by directly seeking happiness because that leaves you too self-centered. It is still all about you at that point, although you don't know it yet. "I'm going to be happy today" we think. And maybe you've had days like that, where you realize that you are trying too hard. It is too self-conscious, it's too intentional. Ego consciousness is still steering the ship.

Remember what I said earlier about the old mammalian brain. Deep contentment is something you drop into—not anything that you consciously work too hard toward. Have you noticed how the happiness of a goal achieved rather quickly passes, and all you do is create another supposedly higher goal? There is an inherent restlessness—and defeat—in the conscious seeking of happiness. Happiness is much more in the realm of gift and surprise, like an alighting dove or a tongue of fire, which is surely why these metaphors are used for the Holy Spirit.

Happiness is too often selfishly defined, and thus it never works for long. We first, like children, define happiness in a largely sensory way, like a satisfying meal or a beautiful hotel room or a wonderful sexual experience, which is all understandable. But those things, of themselves, do not make you happy. If you don't bring happiness into the hotel room, you're not going to be happy. You'll just be pleased for a few minutes. But if you are already happy, you can be in a mediocre hotel room, or even in a not-so-nice hotel room, and you'll still be able to say, "I'm happy and content today."

Sometimes simple things can give you even more and deeper happiness, precisely because you know you are drawing upon a deeper well and stream—and it can be accessed all the time, even without a five-star meal or fantastic sex.

Happiness is always a gift from first seeking union or love. *If love is your actual and constant goal, you can never really fail*, and happiness comes much easier and more naturally. Please think about that, and you will know it is true.

The purifying goal of mysticism is divine union and nothing less. The goal of prayer is divine union—union with what is, with the moment, with yourself, with the divine, which means with everything. Such things as healing, growth, and happiness are admittedly wonderful byproducts of prayer, but they must not be your primary concern. It pollutes the process. So you don't want to make the goal of mysticism or prayer your personal happiness. That keeps you as the reference point: "I want to be happy." This important purification of motivation is quite central, and because we have not insisted on it, we have a lot of church involvement being nothing more than very well disguised self-interest (high premium fire insurance), and not the love of God at all.

As a priest, I am aware that most of the official prayers in the Catholic Sacramentary are praying in some form "That I might go to heaven." Don't believe me? Check it out. As if there is no higher concern or greater need in the world than for my personal eternal livelihood! I do not know how priests continue to recite such self-centered and individualistic prayers day after day. If the rule is true that "*lex orandi est lex credendi*" (the way you pray becomes the form of your belief), then it is no wonder that the Christian people have such a poor record of concern for the suffering of the world, and have themselves initiated so many of the wars and injustices on this earth. We did not teach them how to pray!

You must first seek union itself with God, and with everything, and then the butterfly will most assuredly alight gently and firmly on your shoulder. Then happiness comes along as a wonderful corollary and conclusion, as a gift, as a rich icing on the now well-baked cake of life itself.

Five

The Path to Non-Dual Thinking

*"There is a kind of existence in which epiphanies
and busyness, death and life, God and not—all these
apparent antinomies are merged and made into
one awareness. I am a long way from realizing
such perception myself, but I have lifted the lens to
my eyes."*

—CHRISTIAN WIMAN, poet and
author of *My Bright Abyss*

How do we learn to move away from dualistic thinking? And how do we learn non-dualistic thinking or contemplation?

That is a good question, because we do have to learn it. Dualistic thinking is so taken for granted in the Western world that we just call it thinking. And any systematic teaching of contemplation has been lost to the Western churches for most of five centuries. No wonder we keep splitting into eventually thirty thousand groups that call themselves Christian. We lost the superior mind and heart, or at least our ability to access it. No wonder Jesus said, "Be careful how you listen" (Luke 8:18).

We are all educated into dualistic thinking. We think being

able to make distinctions is what it means to be intelligent or rational. Most of our college professors love to make distinctions for us and teach us how to do the same. We have lost the older tradition that said that there are some things previous to—and even more important than—the making of distinctions. In fact, the distinguishing of everything from other things is part of the problem! Distinctions are largely made in the mind, with words, and that surely has many, many positive and necessary aspects. But it also carries a bit of untruth with it, because you would do well to first see the similarities and deep identities of things before you distinguish this from that. I like to say you must start with "yes" and never with "no."

Even ancient religion saw that its job was to introduce people to an alternative way of thinking, which might have been called shamanism or divining. The practicing of that other way of thinking we would now call meditation, contemplation, or just prayer. I am convinced it is what the original word *prayer* meant. You must use a different processor; you do not fully process the moment by judging it, analyzing it, differentiating it. You do not need to make it special or oppositional. You first must respect anything for being exactly what it is before you adjust it with your mind according to your likes and dislikes. Like a clean mirror, you just reflect it back without any added distortion (read "judgments").

I think people in earlier centuries, before the printing press, before the huge productivity of words, living in an agrarian society perhaps, had much easier access to non-dual thinking. Now we have strobe-light-flashing minds. We do not have easy access to the contemplative mind anymore. It takes more work than ever to get a clean mirror, and it is for that very reason that the work is so important. Few have been taught how.

Catholicism—and Eastern Orthodoxy even more so—have a long tradition of teaching contemplation, and yet I am very often today invited by Protestants to teach it. It is because they know they do not know. They know they never had it in their history or tradition. It was lost by then. We Catholics are in a worse state: We think that because we know the word *contemplation* we also know how to do it. Even Catholic contemplative religious orders stopped teaching it to their own members, which was quite a loss indeed. Many must have lived very frustrated lives, although some learned it by pure grace, by love, and by suffering.[16]

Catholics and Orthodox Christians have to retrieve their own tradition of this alternative consciousness. But most traditionalists today are not traditional at all! They know so little about the Big Tradition themselves, beyond the last four or five hundred years and usually only the last hundred years or even their own lifetimes. That is what happens when you move into a defensive posture against others. You circle the wagons around externals and non-essentials, and the first thing to go is anything interior or subversive to your own ego.

First we have to know that we do have this contemplative tradition. It is very clear in the Desert Fathers and Mothers, in Celtic Christianity, in the Eastern Church's *Philokalia* and Evagrius, in the monastic history of all the ancient orders, which sometimes taught it directly or indirectly (Dionysius, John Cassian, the famous monastery of St. Victor in Paris, Bonaventure, and Francisco de Osuna). Most of our mystics exemplified it more than they could actually verbalize what had happened. Maybe this is part of why we lost it, and why good theological and spiritual teaching is important.

We know non-dual consciousness was taught on the systematic level until as late as the eleventh and twelfth centuries, usually among Benedictines or Cistercians. The early Franciscans are still the beneficiaries of this more ancient understanding, the Rhineland Dominicans beautifully exemplify it, and the Carmelites regather much of it from their ancient history in Palestine at Mount Carmel. Its final flower, even supernova of expression, is, of course, in Teresa of Avila and John of the Cross in the sixteenth century, who had to re-teach contemplation at great costs.

But after the fights of the Reformation, after the over-rationalization of the seventeenth- and eighteenth-century Enlightenment, we became very defensive, and we wanted to prove we were smart and could win arguments. In such a conversation, we by and large took on a more rational form of thinking and covered it with pious Christian words. Our own doctrines were henceforth presented in a dualistic, argumentative, and apologetic way. It was not non-dual consciousness anymore, but entirely dualistic thinking about Christian doctrines! Most priests were educated this way until the much needed reforms of Vatican II in the 1960s.

At this point, after almost five centuries of *not* systematically teaching or even understanding contemplation, we have to find schools, teachers, books, and develop a practice to unlearn the old mind. Most of us thought that contemplatives were just introverted, quiet types who liked to pray. It left us extroverts and doing types out in the cold. Once we begin to learn the contemplative mind, we realize it is almost the natural way of seeing—and we have unlearned it! It is quite natural, as we see in children before the age of six or seven when they start judging and analyzing and distinguishing things one from another.

In my case, I first experienced contemplation before I learned how to name it well or to recognize it as such. I sometimes thought I was being naïve or a foolish Franciscan, not taking my intellect seriously enough. Yet so many smart people in the church frankly felt unspiritual. I do not know how else to say it. Beginning with Thomas Merton's teaching, it has flowered in many of us for the last twenty-five years. Learning from teacher after teacher, from many traditions, I began to name and understand my own experience. If something is this true, then you know for sure that many people will have discovered it, even if they use different vocabularies or have different assumptions about its goal.

I think many come to the contemplative mind as the fruit of suffering or great love. They simply find themselves thinking non-dually, non-oppositionally, and in a non-argumentative way. They enjoy the inner peace of God. They come to know that they can enjoy God, enjoy life, enjoy themselves, and do not need to pick fights in their brain. It is such a pleasant place to live. Read Philippians 2:1–5 where the non-dual mind is on full display, and it leads St. Paul to quote the wonderful hymn of verses 6–11, where he advises that we have "the same mind which is in Christ Jesus." I believe the contemplative mind is the mind of Christ.

The Gospel Is about an Alternative Mind and Thus Alternative Behavior

I often use the term "alternative orthodoxy," a phrase I gained from my Franciscan tradition, having to do with our emphasis upon lifestyle more than verbal correctness. Francis wanted us to *do* the Gospel, to live lives that were simple, loving, joyful, nonviolent. But I believe the reason we lost this alternative orthodoxy is because we first lost our alternative consciousness! We read everything in terms of a kind of dualistic conformity with one side of most questions, which kept us in the world of words—instead of our own experience—and it usually did not emphasize actual practice, which some call "orthopraxy." The contemplative mind does not hide behind words, but is in immediate contact with reality, with people, with events—*as they are*—and without ideological analysis.

Alternative consciousness is largely letting go of my mind's need to solve problems, to fix people, to fix myself, to rearrange the moment because it is not to my liking.

When that mind goes, another mind is already there waiting, already quietly in place. That is what I mean by an alternative consciousness, an alternative set of glasses through which you can see the moment. But you cannot experience the one without letting go of the other—at least for a while. For many people, for most people who have thought dualistically all their life, it feels like dying, it feels like losing, it feels like letting go of my control, which is exactly why our Catholic mystics consistently called it "darkness" or "knowing by darkness." This is surely why a lot of people do not go to higher or more mature stages of prayer. They want light and not darkness. They like to think, and thinking is largely commenting and arguing in your brain, arguing between conflicting ideas or competing ideas. But note that I said you must let go of your dualistic mind at least for a while. You eventually have to return there to get most ordinary jobs done, but even those you will now do in a less compulsive or driven way.

I think the genius of the Dalai Lama and Buddhism is that they do not get lost in metaphysics and argumentation about dogmas and doctrines; they just do not go there. As the Dalai Lama says, "My religion is kindness; my only religion is kindness." We could dismiss that as mere lightweight thinking, until we remember that Jesus said the same, "This is my commandment: You must love one another." It is our religion, too, or at least it should have been.

The Dalai Lama is not saying anything we do not already know, at least on some level. People said the same thing about Mother Teresa—she would just offer simple little one-liners, and people would go away quoting her or saying she changed their life! Contemplation leads you to have simple clear eyes, common-sense faith, and loving energy that makes whatever you say quite compelling. Ironically, it also allows you to deal with often complex issues with the same simplicity and forthrightness, as we now see in Pope Francis.

But that is why we all need to encounter people who are able to operate as an example, a model. The East has always recognized that transmission of spirituality takes place through living models, whom they called gurus, sanyassis, pandits, or avatars. It is what Catholics and Orthodox mean by saints. You cannot just get the good news through concepts, ideas, and theories.

You need to see and feel a living incarnation. "She is doing it. He exemplifies it. It is therefore possible for me, too." It is almost more a taste, a smell, or a touch than an idea. Recent Christianity has relied far, far too much on ideas instead of living models. Sincere Christians can smell holiness, even when the words might seem unorthodox. They can also smell unholiness even from people who do it all perfectly!

So what I am saying here is that it can work the other way around, too; alternative behavior also helps create the alternative mind. *We do not think ourselves into a new way of living, but we live ourselves into new ways of thinking* is one of our core principles at our Living School of Action and Contemplation in Albuquerque, New Mexico.

It is very interesting that in the Eastern Church, most bishops and teachers, and many priests, were monks first. People like Gregory of Nyssa, Gregory Nazianen, Gregory Palamas, Basil, Athanasius, Cyril, and Evagrius Ponticus come to mind. In other words, first living it with some seriousness gave you the authority to talk about it! This is an emphasis that we might well rediscover in our time. Most of us are ordained today without a single instance of having brought another person to faith, hope, or love. Right words can get you ordained. And we have thus far been totally unsuccessful in getting a single seminary of any denomination to have a contemplative emphasis or curriculum.

Every time the Church divided—between East and West, and again as a result of the Reformation—we lost part of the whole message, at least that is how I see it. Further, in subsequent centuries, the neglected parts of the Gospel had to take shape in totally separate denominations which, thank God, preserved some gems, but usually missed some others. I think of the Mennonites, the Quakers, the Amish, the Waldensians, the Pentecostals, and even the Recovery Movement and the Course in Miracles, both of which preserved the very real necessity of forgiveness and healing. I wonder if any one denomination will ever be able to preserve all aspects of the great mind of Christ. Maybe human nature is only prepared to pay attention to a few select things.

Whenever you see a movement into solitude or hermitage or quiet or any kind of aloneness, you know you have non-dual contemplative consciousness reemerging. You cannot spend days, weeks, and months alone unless your mind is different. The dualistic mind goes angry and crazy and bored with that much silence and solitude. The non-dual mind cannot get enough of it. Whenever you see the reemergence of hermits, anchorites, and divisions in orders taking place over how to pray, you know that non-dual consciousness has been rediscovered. Note this pattern especially in the Benedictines, Carmelites, Augustinians, and Franciscans. It is at the core of every break and reform in these orders, although sometimes the interior poverty that contemplation demands gets confused with fights over external poverty in all of these groups—whether you were shod or discalced, or how much you fasted, etc. This is a common mistake.

In sixteenth-century Spain, we have a lesser-known Franciscan friar and spiritual teacher, Francisco de Osuna, teaching Teresa of Avila this contemplative way. She called him her "greatest teacher." She said, before she discovered him, mental prayer, which is what they called it then, was driving her crazy because she knew she could not control this compulsive repetitive obsessive thing that we call thinking. They still called it mental prayer when I was a novice in 1961, but it was largely about concentrating, which, of course, does not work. Most gave up on prayer very early—without realizing that they had. I am surprised more did not leave religious life.

Our Father Francis shows all the evidence of being a supreme contemplative. Even to the first generation of Franciscans who loved him, many like Brother Elias did not know what they were going to do with him. Francis was so simple and naïve to their dualistic way of thinking, yet there was an inner core of friars that accompanied him to the carceri and hermitages for needed structural protection. These were probably Brothers Leo, Giles, Masseo, and Rufino, and maybe even Juniper.

Then we have the intellectual masters, like Bonaventure and Duns Scotus who can maintain their simplicity while also giving the contemplative mind some intellectual rigor. There you have the best of both worlds, at least for educated people. Chapter seven of Bonaventure's *Journey of the Soul into God* (*Itinerarium Mentis ad Deum*) is a very succinct summary of what we now call Centering Prayer or the contemplative mind. So it is in our tradition, but less so in the last four hundred years. People only discovered it by grace and accident, and, thank God, there are usually quiet hidden examples of such enlightenment in every community I have ever worked with.

After the big so-called Enlightenment of the seventeenth and eighteenth centuries we had no room for contemplation because you really looked naïve, like you were just a non-critical thinker, a pious lay brother. Social prayer of the Office and the Divine Liturgy pretty much held the Catholics and religious together in their respective groups, and unfortunately it often became both a substitute and even an avoidance of an actual inner life. Daily Mass was our prayer, and that became sentimentalized and dressed up, and often became high theater to offer us a pseudo feeling of communion, intimacy, and mystery. These are the very gifts that are offered generously in contemplation, but in a way that goes deep and that lasts.

Appendix

A Time Line of Mysticism

2500 BC: First appearances of a sense of a loving personal relationship with God: India and Egypt, Owen Barfield's "Original Participation"

2000–1200 BC: Abraham, Jacob, Elijah in Israel, Early Hinduism

500 BC: "The Axial Age," according to Karl Jaspers; Buddhism is born; Socrates in Greece; Plato; the Upanishads in India

200 BC: Patanjali, Yoga Sutras in India, Jewish Apocalypticism, Book of Psalms, Song of Songs

30 BC: Philo of Alexandria, a Jew in the Diaspora

1st Century: Jesus of Nazareth, as the first non-dual teacher for the West; Paul's Letters, John's Gospel, "Present and final participation" is promised and exemplified, which thrills Western civilization!

2nd Century: Clement of Alexandria first uses the word *mysticus*/hidden

3rd Century: Origin (Father of the Church), Plotinus (Roman philosopher)

4th Century: Basil and the Gregorys in Turkey; Evagrius Ponticus; Augustine; Cassian; Macarius the Great; Desert Fathers and Mothers in Egypt, Syria, Cappadocia/Asia Minor, and Palestine; Trinitarian thinking is possible and highly valued (The "Principle of three" allows and teaches non-dual thinking)

6th Century: Benedict (organizes the possibility), Pseudo Dionysius (apophatic way), Gregory the Great; Buddhism, Lao-Tzu and Taoism (Tao-Te-Ching) spread in China

7th Century: John Climacus, Maximus the Confessor: "Hesychasm" gives Orthodox Christianity a strong mystical basis; Theosis/divinization; Zen Buddhism in Japan and Tibetan Buddhism

8th Century: Rabia (Islamic woman in Iraq), Sankara in India

9th Century: Little happening in Western Christianity, which appears to be dying along with the Roman Empire, except for Celtic monks outside the Empire, who begin to evangelize the continent

10th Century: Symeon the New Theologian in the East

12th Century: Hugh and Richard of St. Victor, Aelred of Rievaulx, Bernard of Clairvaux, Hildegard of Bingen, William of St. Thierry (monastery-based)

13th Century: Explosion of Mysticism: Francis and Clare, Rumi, Meister Eckhart, Beguines and Beghards, Bonaventure, Gertrude, Mechtilde, Hadewijch, Giles of Assisi, Angela of Foligno, Raymond Lull, Richard Rolle, many Franciscan Hermits, German Dominicans Henri Suso and Johannes Tauler, Ibn 'Arabi (Sufi master teacher)

14th Century: Jan Ruysbroeck, Gregory Palamas, Hafiz, Cloud of Unknowing, Julian of Norwich, Catherine of Siena, Catherine of Genoa, Walter Hilton, Thomas à Kempis

15th Century: Nicholas of Cusa (coincidence of opposites), Francisco de Osuna, Kabir (both Hindu and Sufi holy man), Nicholas von der Flue

16th Century: The Final Supernova! Ignatius of Loyola, Teresa of Avila, John of the Cross, Francis de Sales, Jacob Boehme, Erasmus. (Yet most church reformations are born of extreme dualistic consciousness.)

17th Century: Crisis and Decline: Sweet piety or reason as a substitute for contemplation; the Enlightenment presented as the full triumph of dualistic thought; the Desert of Non-Participation begins, according to Owen Barfield; we have Brother Lawrence, George Fox, Blaise Pascal, and many women mystics who never attained prominence precisely because they were women and not taken seriously or allowed to be literate

18th Century: Jean Pierre de Caussade, Baal-Shem-Tov, John Wesley, Seraphim of Sarov, Emmanuel Swedenborg, Hasidic Judaism, William Blake

19th Century: Therese of Lisieux, Charles De Foucauld, Henry David Thoreau, and William Wordsworth (the nature mystics)

20th Century: Rediscovery of Participation: Friedrich von Hugel, Gandhi, Evelyn Underhill, Thomas Kelly, Howard Thurman, Suzuki, Bede Griffiths, Rainer Maria Rilke, Elizabeth of the Trinity, Martin Luther King, Alan Watts, Simone Weil, Thomas Merton, Thich Nhat Hanh, Rinzai Zen, Martin Buber, Etty Hillesum, Dag Hammarskjold, Anthony de Mello, Ken Wilber, Gerald May, Ramana Maharshi, Teilhard de Chardin, Hugo Enomiya-Lassalle, Abraham Heschel, Tagore, Ruth Barrows, John Main, Eckhart Tolle, Bernadette Roberts, Paramahansa Yogananda, various rinpoches and gurus, Henri Le Saux, Karl Rahner, Helen Keller, Mother Teresa, Dalai Lama (admittedly an arguable and incomplete list, that some will find fault with on one issue or another).

What is emerging is a major first-time interface between East and West, the "two hemispheres of the Body of Christ": a re-discovery of non-dual thinking, acting, reconciling, boundary crossing, and bridge building—based on the inner experience of God.

A *Second Axial Age* might just be emerging. Yes, some is immature, some is syncretistic, some is ungrounded, some not integrated, but the steps toward maturity are always and necessarily immature. The Holy Spirit is still evolving consciousness and teaching us how to pray.

Notes

1. *Nostra Aetate* (*Declaration on the Relation of the Church to Non-Christian Religions*), 1, 2.

2. *Nostra Aetate*, 1, 2.

3. Augustine of Hippo, *Retractions,* 1:13.3.

4. *Optatam Totius* (Decree on the Training of Priests), 15.

5. Aldous Huxley, *The Perennial Philosophy* (New York: Harper & Brothers, 1945), vii.

6. Julian of Norwich, *The Showings of Divine Love*, chapter 9.

7. Julian of Norwich, *The Showings of Divine Love*, chapter 65.

8. Julian of Norwich, *The Showings of Divine Love*, chapter 51.

9. Richard Rohr, O.F.M., *The Naked Now* (New York: Crossroad, 2009), chapter sixteen.

10. Cynthia Bourgeault, "The Shape of God," conference on the Trinity by Cynthia Bourgeault and Richard Rohr, O.F.M.

11. Karl Rahner, S.J., *The Trinity* (New York: Crossroad, 1999), 10.

12. *The Naked Now,* chapter two.

13. Richard Rohr, O.F.M., *Falling Upward* (San Francisco: Jossey-Bass, 2011), chapter three.

14. Richard Rohr, O.F.M., and others, "What Is the Emerging Church," audio recording, Center for Action and Contemplation.

15. Richard Rohr, O.F.M., *The Naked Now*, chapters four through six.

16. Richard Rohr, O.F.M., *The Naked Now,* chapter sixteen.

Sources

Introduction
Excerpted from Richard Rohr, *Oneing: An Alternative Orthodoxy*, vol. I, no. I, introduction.

Chapter One
Excerpted from Richard Rohr, "Finding God in the Depths of Silence," Festival of Faiths, talk presented at the Actors Theater of Louisville, Louisville, Kentucky, May 15, 2013.

Chapter Two
Excerpted from Richard Rohr and respondents, "Sacred Silence: Pathway to Compassion," Festival of Faiths, talk presented at the Galt House, Louisville, Kentucky, Saturday, May 18, 2013.

Chapter Three
Excerpted from Richard Rohr, Festival of Faiths, talk presented Sunday, May 19, 2013. After the remarks of Father Rohr and other presenters, His Holiness the Dalai Lama delivered a talk on Silent Compassion at the Yum Center in Louisville, Kentucky. This talk, approved ahead of time by the Dalai Lama's committee, was deemed to be a true statement from the Christian Tradition, but also one with which other faiths could agree.

Chapter Four
Excerpted from Mark Lombard's *St. Anthony Messenger*

magazine October 2012 interview with Father Richard Rohr immediately following the conference in Santa Fe, New Mexico, which Rohr led on "Franciscan Mysticism: I Am That Which I Am Seeking."

Chapter Five

Excerpted from Susan Hines-Brigger's interview of Father Richard Rohr, *St. Anthony Messenger* magazine, at the Festival of Faiths, May 2013.

Appendix

Presented by Richard Rohr, O.F.M., at the January 2010 conference "Following the Mystics through the Narrow Gate . . . Seeing God in All Things."

DISCOVER MORE OF
RICHARD ROHR

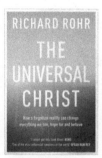

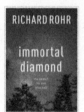

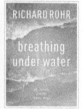

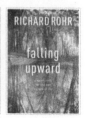